The First Christmas

CHEX BOOKS NEW YORK

Long ago, in a town called
Nazareth, there lived a young
woman named Mary. One day
a great light appeared and
the angel Gabriel stood before her.
"Do not be afraid," said the angel.
"I bring you joyful news.
God has chosen you to be
the mother of his son. You will
have a baby and you must
call him Jesus."

In the same town there lived
a carpenter named Joseph.
Joseph loved Mary very much.
He was going to marry her.
The angel came to visit Joseph
and told him that Mary was going
to have God's son. Later that day
Joseph came to see Mary and told
her what the angel had said.

One day a message came from
the governor of the land.
All of the people had to go back
to the place where they had been
born so they could be counted.
Joseph was worried. He and Mary
would have to go to Bethlehem.
This was a long way away
and Mary was almost ready
to have her baby.

They set off early the next morning.
Joseph led the way. Mary rode
on a donkey. The road was
long and hard. They didn't reach
Bethlehem until the evening.
The town was full of people.
Joseph tried everywhere to find
a place to stay, but all the rooms
were taken.
Mary was so tired she could hardly
stay awake.

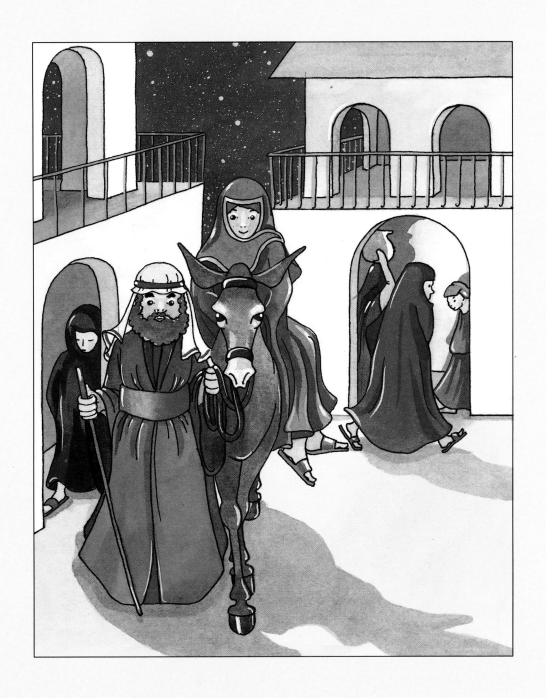

At last an innkeeper said,
"All my rooms are full, but you
can use my stable. It is clean
and warm in there."
Joseph thanked him and they went
inside. All around them cows and
donkeys lay peacefully asleep.
The hay was soft and smelled sweet.
Mary and Joseph lay down and rested.

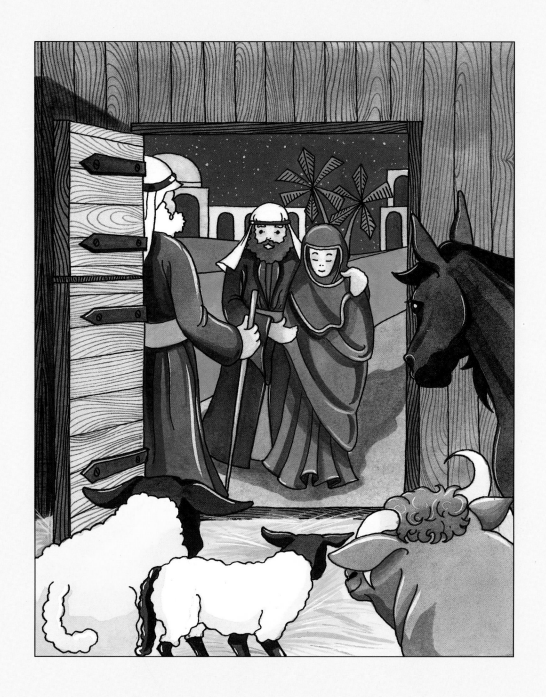

In the night, Mary gave birth to
her baby. It was a boy as
the angel had said. They named
him Jesus.
Mary wrapped him in a blanket
and laid him in a manger, where
it was soft and warm.
Mary and Joseph watched over
Jesus lovingly. They knew he was
a very special baby.

Out on the hillside above
the town, some shepherds were
looking after their sheep.
Suddenly the sky was filled with
light and an angel appeared.
The shepherds fell to the ground
in fear.
But the angel said, "Do not be
afraid. I bring you good news.
Today a child is born. He is the
son of God. You will find him in
Bethlehem, lying in a manger."

The shepherds gazed in wonder
as the sky was filled with angels
singing.
"We must go and find this child,"
said one. "We can take one of our
newborn lambs as a gift."
They went to Bethlehem and found
Jesus in the stable with Mary and
Joseph. They fell to their knees
and offered their gift.

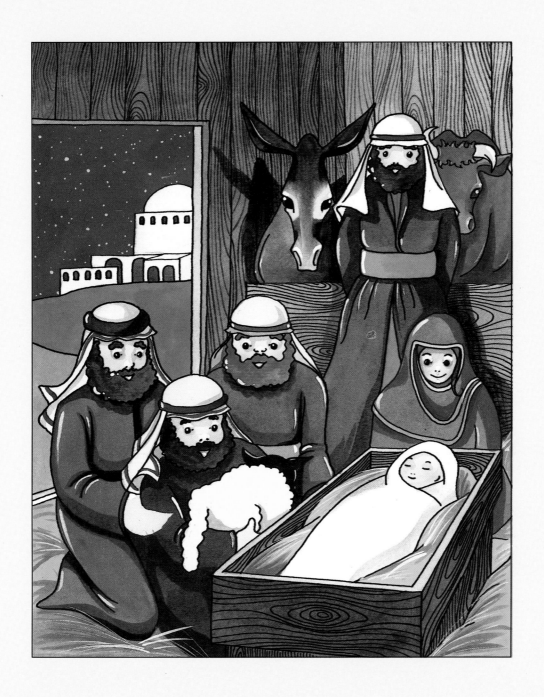

Far away in an eastern land
lived three wise men. One night
they saw a bright new star in
the sky. They wanted to know
what it meant. They looked in
their books for the answer.
"It means that a new king
has been born," they said.
"We must go and look for him
so that we can worship him.
The star will guide us."

They set off on their journey.
The star shone brightly in front
of them by day and by night.
They came to the palace of King
Herod. He was not very pleased
when he heard about the new king.
''Go and find him, so that
I can worship him, too,'' said Herod.
He really wanted to find Jesus
so that he could kill him.

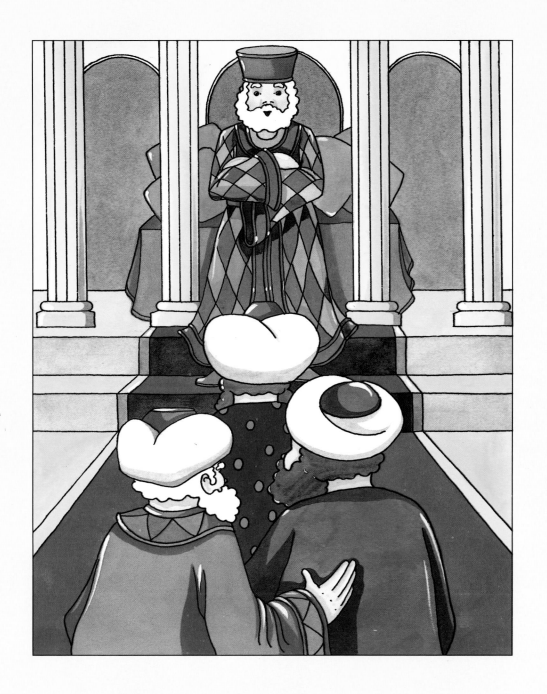

The three wise men followed
the star for many miles.
It stopped right over the stable
where Jesus lay. "We are looking
for the newborn king," they said.
"A bright star has guided us
from far away."
Joseph led them into the stable.
They knelt before Jesus and
offered him some very special
gifts of gold, frankincense
and myrrh.

The next day, the wise men set out for King Herod's palace. They stopped to rest and while they were asleep an angel came to them in a dream.

"Do not go back to Herod," the angel warned. "He wants to kill Jesus."

The wise men decided to go home a different way.

Mary and Joseph were very happy and proud. They knew their baby was really the son of God. They knew he was very special and that he would have important work to do when he grew up. They also knew that Jesus would be loved throughout the world and that people would remember his birth as a time of happiness and peace.

Say these words again

town	full
angel	stable
carpenter	baby
God	manger
message	singing
tired	lamb
find	gold